The Revolutionary War

VOLUME 1

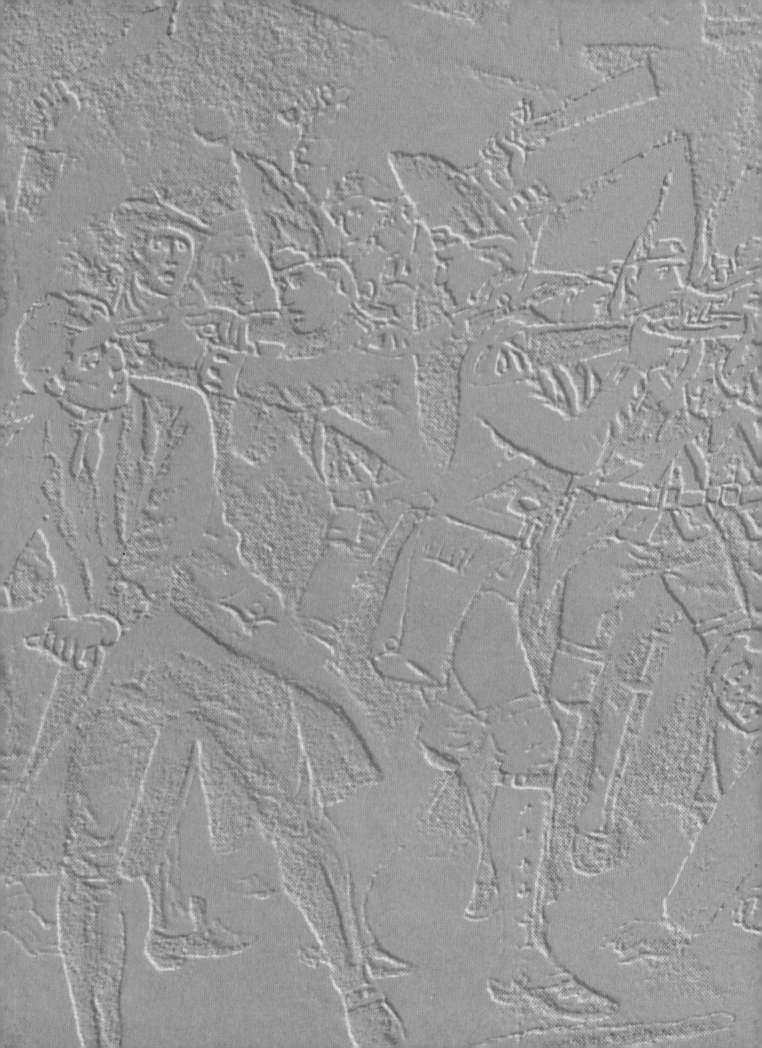

⚜ The ⚜
Revolutionary War

VOLUME 1
The Road to Rebellion

James R. Arnold & Roberta Wiener

GROLIER
EDUCATIONAL

**Published in 2002
by Grolier Educational**

Grolier Publishing Company,
90 Sherman Turnpike,
Danbury, Connecticut 06816

Website address: http://publishing.grolier.com

Library of Congress Cataloging-in-Publication Data

The Revolutionary War.
     p. cm.
  Contents: v. 1. The road to rebellion—v. 2. The shot heard around the world—v. 3. Taking up arms—v. 4. The spirit of 1776—v. 5. 1777: a year of decision—v. 6. the road to Valley Forge—v. 7. War of attrition—v. 8. The American cause in peril—v. 9. The turn of the tide —v. 10. An independent nation.
     Includes bibliographical references and indexes.
     ISBN 0-7172-5553-0 (set)—ISBN 0-7172-5554-9 (v. 1)—
ISBN 0-7172-5555-7 (v. 2)—ISBN 0-7172-5556-5 (v. 3)—
ISBN 0-7172-5557-3 (v. 4)—ISBN 0-7172-5558-1 (v. 5)—
ISBN 0-7172-5559-X (v. 6)—ISBN 0-7172-5560-3 (v. 7)—
ISBN 0-7172-5561-1 (v. 8)—ISBN 0-7172-5562-X (v. 9)—
ISBN 0-7172-5563-8 (v. 10)
     1. United States—History—Revolution, 1775–1783—Juvenile literature. [1. united States—History—Revolution. 1775–1783.]
     I. Grolier Incorporated.

E208 .R47 2002
973.3—dc21   2001018998

Printed and bound in Singapore

CONTENTS

Introduction

IN 1774 AMERICAN LEADERS came to Philadelphia. They had something important to discuss. At the time all Americans were subjects of the world's most powerful nation, Great Britain. That was about to change.

The men came to attend a meeting, or congress. They called themselves delegates of the United Colonies in Congress. The delegates represented all thirteen American colonies except Georgia. The delegates resented Great Britain's control of their lives. They thought that Americans did not have the same rights as other British subjects. So, they adopted a declaration of personal rights, including the rights of life, liberty, and property. They did not know that to win these rights they would have to fight a war.

History calls this war by two names. The most common name is the War of the American Revolution, or the Revolutionary War for short. The conflict is also known as the War for American Independence. Each name for the war contains an important word.

Revolution means the overthrow of a government. Sometimes revolutions that try to overthrow a government are peaceful. More often they involve violence. In the case of the Revolutionary War the violence lasted seven long years from 1775 until 1781.

Independence means freedom from control. In the War for American Independence American citizens fought to escape from the control of Great Britain.

Let us return for a moment to the delegates who came to Philadelphia in 1774. They included some of the great men in American history. We will learn about many of them, such as George Washington and John Adams. And, as we will learn, many delegates were very smart. But no one can clearly predict the future. Neither Washington nor Adams nor anyone else knew that 1774 would be the last year of peace. However, the delegates did know that they were beginning a risky journey.

When people revolt against a government, they believe they are fighting for freedom. In other words, they are fighting for an idea. They believe that this idea is good. They believe that they are on the right side. They believe that their cause is just.

A government thinks very differently. A government calls the people who attack it outlaws because they are acting illegally, or outside of the law. Another word for this special kind of outlaw is rebel. A government calls on its people to stay loyal. Then it uses force to crush the rebels.

During the Revolutionary War both sides believed that their cause was just. The Americans who rebelled called themselves patriots. The British government called them traitors. When two sides disagree so powerfully, it is very hard to avoid fighting.

Yet many Americans and Britons did not want to fight. Some hoped that leaders could just talk about their differences and then make a peaceful agreement. Many others simply wanted to be left alone. Think of the people living in the thirteen colonies as being divided into three equal groups. Probably one of these groups, one-third of all Americans, was neutral. That means these people did not want to fight on either side.

The remaining two groups, two-thirds of all Americans, disagreed with one another. One group listened to the British government and chose to remain loyal. They were known as loyalists, or Tories. The other group chose to fight against Great Britain.

There were probably as many Tories as there were rebels. Sometimes they were neighbors. Often they were friends. When the war began, they had to fight one another. So the Revolutionary War saw fighting between the rebels and the British government and fighting between the rebels and the Tories. In this way the war was also a civil war. As we will see, some of the hardest fighting involved American rebels fighting American loyalists. Also, sadly, during this fighting Americans inflicted some of the war's worst cruelties on other Americans.

It is hard for people living today to understand how this could be. Every July 4 we celebrate Independence Day. It is a happy holiday with picnics, games, and fireworks. But July 4 is most important because it celebrates something that happened on July 4, 1776. On that date American leaders delivered the Declaration of Independence. Many of those leaders are the same men who came to Philadelphia in 1774 as delegates of the *United Colonies in Congress*. This congress went down in history as the *First Continental Congress*.

Let us begin our study of the Revolutionary War, the War for American Independence, by learning about the lifetime experiences of the Americans who were alive in 1774. History is the study of what has happened in the life of a group of people. By learning some of the history that took place before the Revolutionary War, we will be able to understand how the war began. We will be able to understand what the delegates who came to Philadelphia in 1774 were talking about. We will understand why the delegates thought the way they did. We will understand why they were willing to risk fighting a war for independence.

CHAPTER ONE

Life in the American Colonies

During the years before the Revolutionary War the American colonies became more prosperous and economically important. They also grew more culturally different and politically independent from Great Britain.

Great Britain had thirteen colonies in North America. The first Europeans to settle and survive in the part of **America** that became the thirteen **colonies** arrived in the spring of 1607. A group of English colonists, 100 men and 4 boys, landed at Jamestown, Virginia. Six months later only 38 of them were still living. The rest had starved, died of disease, or been killed in fights with Indians. The next year 70 more settlers, including two women, arrived from England. Many struggles lay ahead. But by the time of the American Revolution Virginia was the largest and richest colony.

Anyone who traveled from Europe to the **New World** had to endure a voyage of several months in a crowded sailing ship tossed around by the sea. Poor food, sickness, and foul weather plagued many voyages. Yet the promise of wealth and freedom, particularly freedom of religion, lured settlers to the New World. Over the next 150 years Dutch, Swedish, German, and Scottish settlers followed the English to the colonies.

From Pennsylvania northward most colonists lived on family farms and produced much of what they needed. They produced extra crops or livestock to sell so they could buy the items they didn't produce for themselves. They were an independent people. Few were willing to work for others when they could work for themselves on

America: usually refers to the United States of America, but really means the land that contains the continents of North America, and South America

colony: a land that is owned and controlled by a particular nation, but is not really a part of that nation; a colonist is a permanent settler of a colony, as opposed to a temporary official sent by the "mother" country that controls the colony

New World/Old World: the New World is the western hemisphere, including North, Central, and South America; the Old World refers to Europe, Asia, and Africa, so called because people in the eastern part of the world did not know the western hemisphere existed until the fifteenth century

Sailing ships carried settlers to the New World. Population grew fast: in 1650 the colonies had about 52,000 people; in 1700 about 250,000; in 1760 about 1,700,000.

West Indies: the islands of the Caribbean Sea, so called because they were once thought to be a part of India

their own land. That is why they left their familiar homes behind and endured months at sea. Once enough people settled in an area, they established villages, businesses, schools, churches, and government.

Cities grew in the north: Boston, Newport, New York, Philadelphia. Each of these cities had a harbor. They became America's most important ports. Ships moved through these ports carrying goods to and from Europe and the **West Indies.** Philadelphia, the largest city in the colonies, had a

population of nearly 40,000 by 1775. It was, after London, the second largest city in the British Empire.

During the colonial period, the years before the Revolution, there was nothing so busy as a harbor town. Every one of the thirteen colonies had a port on the ocean or on a river. Soldiers and sailors, new settlers and merchants came and went. Travelers always needed food and lodging. Goods produced in the colonies or brought from other countries passed through these ports. Ship-builders were kept busy by the constant demand for their work. Fishermen and whalers set sail from the

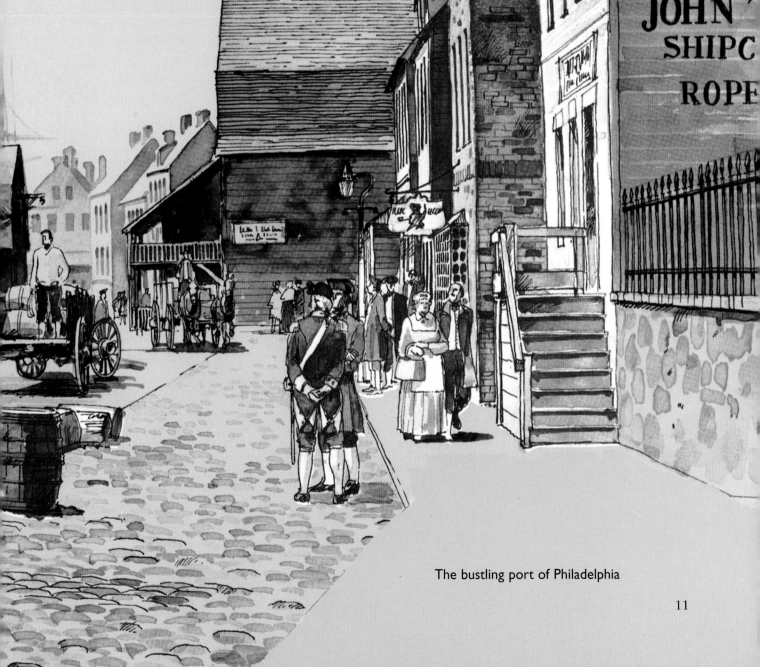

The bustling port of Philadelphia

harbors and returned with their catch. Farmers who lived inland brought grain and flour, livestock and meat to sell. In the northern colonies the most successful traders built up fortunes by shipping fish, lumber, pig iron, rum, and slaves.

As in the northern colonies, most settlers in the southern colonies were farmers. In the south the most successful ones built up large plantations of thousands of acres along the rivers and near the seacoast. Plantations in Maryland and Virginia grew one **cash crop**, tobacco. Tobacco required hard work to grow, and it wore out the soil. To grow a single crop like tobacco successfully, plantation owners depended on slave labor and huge tracts of land. In the Carolinas rice and indigo became the most important cash crops. There too plantation owners used slaves.

> **cash crop:** a crop grown to sell for cash, such as tobacco; as opposed to a crop grown for one's own use, such as vegetables

This advertisement appeared in a Boston newspaper in 1773: "TO BE SOLD—A likely Negro Girl about 8 Years old strong and hearty. Also a strong, hearty Negro Girl about 4 Months old to be given away."

Before the Revolution slavery was legal in all of the colonies. Many white people in both the north and south made money from the slave trade. But slave labor suited the southern climate best. So it was in the south where slavery became important to the colonists' way of life.

Most southern white settlers could neither afford large amounts of land nor slaves. They kept moving westward and occupied the less good lands in the mountains. The small farmers of the south actually outnumbered the wealthy planters, but the planters held most of the political power. Because the population of the south was more widely scattered than in the north, roads, schools, and villages were fewer and farther apart.

Charleston, on the coast of South Carolina, was the most important city in the south. Arriving ships brought slaves to its harbor, and departing ships carried tobacco and rice. Baltimore and Annapolis in Maryland and Savannah in Georgia also became sea ports.

Below: How some of Philadelphia's varied inhabitants dressed in colonial times: from left to right, an upper-class woman, a Quaker merchant, a shopkeeper, a German housewife, and a journeyman printer.

Right: The slave trade moved large numbers of human beings from Africa to America. For the voyage the slaves were chained and packed tightly into ships. The traders packed them in so they would have more people to sell and would make more money at the end of the voyage. Many captives died on the voyages from disease, cold, and starvation. The slave traders did not care. For them it was part of the cost of doing business.

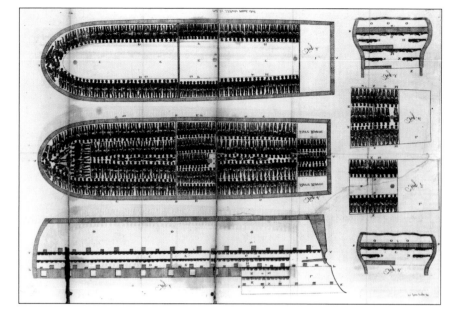

charter: document containing rules for running an organization or government

English laws discouraged all the colonists from making goods by machinery or manufacturing. Instead, England wanted to sell the colonists English-made manufactured goods. As a result the colonies had very little industry. Colonists had small mills for grinding grain into flour and small forges for making simple iron goods, but most everything complicated or fancy came from Europe.

By 1775 the thirteen colonies held two and a half million people. One person of every five was an African slave. Most of the slaves lived in the south, but all of the colonies had some slave owners. The white population had come from many European countries. Many had not been in America for very long when the Revolution began. But they called themselves Americans, and they were all subjects of the Crown. In other words, they were subjects of the English king.

How England Governed the Colonies

Each English colony had its own royal **charter** granted by the king of England. Every colony's charter was different. Each colony had its own legislature with an upper and a lower house, and a system of courts. Through the legislature the colony ran its own civil affairs and collected its own taxes. The king put a royal governor in charge of every colony. The royal governor had the final say over everything the legislature did and when it could meet, and he had the power to appoint whomever he wanted to the upper house. When a legislature passed a law, the governor could either veto it or send to England for approval.

Right: The entrance to Whitehall, the seat of the British government. It was named after the street in London where the government office buildings were located. Because it took a long time for messages to cross the Atlantic Ocean, it was hard for officials in Whitehall to manage affairs in America smoothly.

The governor also appointed all judges and court officials.

These were important powers, but most royal governors used their powers carefully. They saw their job as keeping the peace and keeping out of trouble. Most royal governors were strangers to the colonies they were sent to govern. They were chosen not for their talent and experience, but for their status in England. That made them easy to control when they arrived in the colonies.

As time went on, local people, called provincials because they lived in the provinces, were able to influence royal governors to appoint the men that provincial leaders recommended. The local legislatures took control over the salaries of the royal officials as well.

England also had a legislature, called Parliament, with an upper house and a lower house. They were called the House of Lords and the House of Commons. Over the course of England's history the monarch and Parliament had struggled for power. Past parliaments had arrested and executed kings, and past kings had ordered parliaments to be disbanded, or shut down. The role of

A busy dock on the Thames River, London. Trade with America was important to many English businessmen. Government restrictions on trade with America hurt London's merchants and shippers.

the army and the power of the Catholic and Protestant churches also caused many conflicts in Britain.

In the 1700s the role of prime minister became important in the **British** government. The prime minister got his power from both the king and the parliament. In England only free men who owned land could vote. Only one adult male in four could meet these requirements. The wealthy, upper-class property owners controlled British politics. Because England was a democracy with free speech, many English people criticized both the king and the government.

King George III became king in 1760 when his grandfather, George II, died. He was 22 years old when he became king. He disliked all critics and refused to listen to them. He was very stubborn and stuck to his own opinions with great firmness. In his first ten years on the throne he went through seven different prime ministers, who either resigned or were fired. Because no prime minister stayed in power for long, none of them ever grew strong. Yet the government needed someone strong, and young King George III was a strong ruler. His influence was great during the important years leading up to the Revolution.

Before 1754 England's main interest in the colonies was commercial, which means concerned with making money. Parliament had passed a set of laws that gave England control over trade with her colonies. In most other things the colonies were left to run their own affairs. That way the colonies could produce more wealth and commerce. England's mission was to give protection, peace, and law and order, and to send the ships that carried the goods needed by the settlers. It did not cost England very much to do those things. Benjamin Franklin noted, "The colonies cost England nothing in forts, citadels, garrisons, or armies to keep them in [control]. They were governed at the expense of a little pen, ink, and paper."

When Franklin wrote those words, the relationship between the colonies and England still pleased most Americans. The colonies simply wanted to be left alone to grow and prosper. Americans wanted to be a loyal part of the British **Empire.**

British: the nationality of a person born in Great Britain (England, Scotland, Wales, and Northern Ireland); someone from England is called English

empire: all of the colonies controlled by a particular nation

CHAPTER TWO

The French and Indian War

For a very long time before the Revolutionary War England and France were enemies. Often they waged war against each other. Even during peaceful times they competed fiercely. When British and French settlers came to North America, they brought the conflict with them.

After cutting down trees, the settlers square up the logs to build houses. Indians watch and see that the settlers are changing the land.

As the colonies grew, settlers pushed west to find new land. There were two major barriers blocking them. First there were the people who already lived on the land. These were the people whom the settlers called Indians and whom we today call Native Americans. At the time the first white settlers landed on the shore of Virginia, more than one and a half million American Indians lived on the land that would eventually become the modern United States.

Very few Native Americans welcomed British settlers. Most Indians quickly learned that after the British settlers entered their land, everything changed. The first task of any settler starting a farm was to cut down the trees to build a cabin and to clear land for planting crops. As a result, the thickly wooded lands of the New World were transformed into a patchwork of farms and open fields. Instead of the stone houses of the Old World, the colonists built their houses out of the trees they cut down. The settlers also hunted forest animals,

Between 1689 and 1815 England and France fought six wars. America was in all six wars. King George's War, 1740-48, saw Massachusetts volunteers under Colonel William Pepperell capture the great French fortress of Louisbourg, Nova Scotia.

such as deer, elk, and bear, for food. The clearing of forest land and the increase in the number of hunters quickly made the game animals scarce. Many of the Indians in the east depended on the large animals of the forests for their survival. As the new settlers cut down the forests, the Indians saw their familiar land changing forever and their food supply getting harder to find.

The Native Americans could tolerate the British settlers when there were not too many of them. But the Native Americans saw that the first cabins were like seeds that sprouted to grow more and more cabins. Soon there were too many whites, and the Indians could no longer live in the way they always had. Some Indian tribes still tried to live in peace with the British settlers. Most fought hard to defend their land.

The settlers in turn had to defend themselves. In 1754 there were only five companies of British soldiers, with about 100 men each, in all of America. Each colony had the authority to raise, equip, and train its own militia for protection against the Indians. Colonies such as Rhode Island and Delaware, which were not threatened by Indians, did not keep an active militia.

Indians ambush Braddock's troops in Virginia, 1755.

Young George Washington

George Washington was born on February 22, 1732, in Westmoreland County, in eastern Virginia. February 22 was once celebrated as a national holiday, but it has been replaced by Presidents' Day, which honors both Abraham Lincoln's and George Washington's birthdays.

George Washington's great-grandfather had sailed from England to settle in Virginia in 1657. The Washington family had lived there ever since. George spent most of his childhood on the family plantation, called Ferry Farm, across the Rappahannock River from Fredericksburg, Virginia. The famous story of his chopping down the cherry tree and admitting his wrongdoing is just a legend. So little is known about George Washington's childhood that people felt the need to make something up. He did grow up to be a very honest man, so it was easy to believe that as a boy he once said, "I cannot tell a lie."

George Washington attended local schools now and then between the ages of seven and fifteen. In addition to school subjects such as math and reading, he learned about surveying, growing tobacco, and raising livestock while working on the plantation. When George was eleven, his father died, and George went to live at Mount Vernon with Lawrence, his older half-brother. Lawrence and his wife introduced young George to many interesting and influential people.

George Washington went to work as a surveyor by the time he was sixteen. His work took him into the wilderness of western Virginia, where he developed a lifelong interest in settlement of the West.

When Lawrence died, George inherited Mount Vernon at the age of twenty. Washington enjoyed running the estate and expanded it from 2,500 to 8,000 acres. He was ahead of his time because he knew about crop rotation and soil fertilization. He had also inherited 18 slaves along with Mount Vernon and bought many more, so that by 1760 he had 49 slaves. Still, Washington actually disapproved of slavery and hoped that some day it would be abolished. He fed his slaves well, employed a doctor for them, and refused to sell them and break up their families.

The second barrier that British settlers faced was New France. The first French settlers had entered the lands to the north of the British colonies. There in Canada some acted in the same way as the British settlers. They too cleared land and built cabins, villages, and towns. Over time they built a great capital at Quebec. But there were far fewer French settlers than British settlers. The French did not cause as much change as the British. Their impact on the land was less. That made it easier for the Indians to accept the French.

In addition, many French settlers lived like the Indians. They left the settlements and paddled their canoes westward in order to find good land on which to hunt

George Washington at Mount Vernon before the Revolution, a well-dressed planter among his slaves

George Washington liked many of the forms of entertainment popular among plantation society: parties, plays and concerts, fox-hunting, fishing, horse-racing, billiards, and card games. He was tall and athletic, and an excellent horseman. He liked to dress in fashionable and high-quality clothing. He was a loyal British subject who served in the Virginia House of Burgesses and worked as a justice of the peace for his county.

and trap. They returned to the settlements once a year to trade their furs for bullets and gunpowder. They spent most of their time among the Indians. The French trappers and the Indians got along very well together. As the years passed, the French trappers followed the waterways through the wilderness all the way to the Mississippi River. Since they were the first Europeans to visit the land, they claimed it for their country. The French eventually claimed all America from the Allegheny Mountains to the Rocky Mountains and from Canada to Mexico. The land became New France, a vast country where very few whites lived. A major conflict arose when British settlers tried to claim some of that land.

For a long time British settlers did not venture west of the Allegheny Mountains. In Virginia these mountains stand about 130 miles west of the Atlantic Ocean. The Allegheny Mountains were like a wall. Few English settlers moved past it. Those who did were trappers. Just like the French trappers, they moved about in search of otters and beavers and other fur-bearing animals. British trappers learned that the lands west of the Allegheny Mountains, in the Ohio River valley, were very rich in furs. They began to travel there from western Pennsylvania. Meanwhile, some British traders in Virginia formed the Ohio Company in 1748. Their goal also was to exploit the rich lands to the west. The British monarch, King George II, approved. He thought that the Ohio Company would help his colonies grow bigger.

Naturally, French trappers did not like the British moving west. They built a series of forts to block the British. The French also encouraged the Indians to attack the British. Small battles, or skirmishes, between the British and the French continued until 1753. In that year the royal governor of Virginia, Governor Dinwiddie, sent a 21-year-old man named George Washington to the Ohio River valley to warn the French to withdraw. The French firmly told Washington that they were there to stay.

Like the French trappers, the British needed a base. The next year, 1754, Governor Dinwiddie sent a militia company to build a fort at a good location at the forks of the Ohio River. There the Monongahela River and Allegheny River joined to form the Ohio River. We know the place today as Pittsburgh, Pennsylvania. Before the militia finished their fort, 500 French soldiers and Indians forced them to leave. The French completed the fort and named it Fort Duquesne.

Marching in the direction of Fort Duquesne came Lieutenant-Colonel George Washington and 60 frontiersmen. His mission was to protect the fort builders. Through no fault of his own he arrived too late. He met the defeated fort builders and learned the news of the French attack. Washington continued to a clearing known as Great Meadows. There he heard that a small French force was nearby. Washington led his men in a surprise attack against the French. The Virginians killed

George Washington supervising the raising of the British flag at Fort Necessity.

the French commander and 9 others while capturing 21 prisoners. It was a small triumph that stirred up a hornets' nest of French anger.

Washington had his men build a fort at Great Meadows. The fort's name reflected the desperate situation: Fort Necessity. On July 3, 1754, 500 French and 400 Indians attacked Fort Necessity. Washington and his men resisted as best they could, but the situation was hopeless. The next day Washington surrendered. The French commander allowed Washington and his men to retreat with their weapons. That type of surrender was known as

allowing the loser the honors of war. Surrendering with the honors of war was not considered shameful.

Washington retreated 50 miles over the mountains to the east. There his men built another fort and waited to see what would happen. No one at the time knew how important that little battle in western Pennsylvania would be. The shots fired at Fort Necessity began a world war.

British leaders decided to send a large number of soldiers to North America to fight that war. They also decided to let England's ally, Prussia, do most of the fighting in Europe. French leaders made a different decision. France sent some soldiers to North America, but most of the French attention went elsewhere.

The year after the battle at Fort Necessity, 1755, British forces landed in Virginia. They wanted revenge. A British major-general named Edward Braddock decided to move his forces against the French at Fort Duquesne. George Washington joined Braddock to help guide the British. Braddock assembled

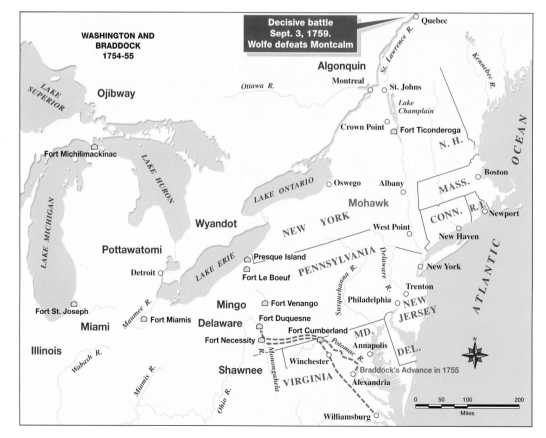

Key

French-Allied Indians in Blue

British-Allied Indians in Red

Washington's Advance in 1754 - - -

Opposite Top: At the age of 21 George Washington began his military career by joining the Virginia militia. He was a stern disciplinarian with his troops and even flogged and hanged deserters. He is shown here as a colonel of the Virginia militia.

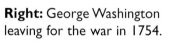

Right: George Washington leaving for the war in 1754.

a powerful army. It included 1,400 British regulars and 1,100 American soldiers from Virginia and Maryland.

Braddock decided to wage war in the same way it was fought in Europe. His army advanced with a large wagon train carrying supplies and baggage. He dragged many artillery pieces along with him. Braddock failed to understand that fighting in the American wilderness was very different from warfare in Europe. He paid for his failure by losing most of his regulars as well as his own life.

That happened when a smaller force of French and Indians ambushed his army as they marched along a narrow cart path. The French and Indians moved and fought as individuals. They spread out to take cover behind trees and rocks. Braddock's people could barely see them in the thick forest. All they could see was a puff of smoke when one of them fired his musket. Meanwhile, Braddock's regulars did what they had been trained to do. They had learned that brave soldiers stood shoulder to shoulder in close formation and moved and fired only when ordered. Since they wore red coats and white crossbelts, they made easy targets. The officers, who wore even showier uniforms, were especially easy to shoot. Sixty-three out of 86 British officers were killed or wounded in that battle.

A French fur trader leads Indians
from Wisconsin and Michigan.
Major-General Braddock,
wounded, falls from his horse,
which is shown being caught by
Washington.

The American soldiers in Braddock's army knew better how to fight in the wilderness. They fought "Indian fashion" by leaving their shoulder-to-shoulder formations and taking cover. The British officers did not understand that way of fighting. They thought the Americans were being cowardly. They ordered the Americans to return to their formations.

After three hours the fight was over. It was a total French victory. At a cost of only 43 French and Indian casualties, 914 men in Braddock's army were casualties. Among them was Braddock. During the fight he showed great courage. Five of his horses were shot out from under him. Finally Braddock fell with a mortal wound. Young George Washington also displayed courage and leadership. Enemy bullets pierced his clothes and killed two horses beneath him. But Washington lived to help organize the retreat of the survivors. A British officer named Thomas Gage joined him in that task.

The mortally wounded Braddock being carried from the site of the ambush by his retreating troops. Braddock's defeat taught some lessons to certain sharp-eyed Americans. Benjamin Franklin was at that time a well-known Pennsylvania newspaper publisher. He later wrote how Braddock's defeat "gave us Americans the first Suspicion" that the famous British regulars could be beaten.

The citizens of Winchester, Virginia, asking George Washington to protect them from Indian attack. Twenty years later this frontier colonel would become the commander-in-chief of the American army.

George Washington and his troops fighting along the Monongahela River. Some men who played important roles in the Revolutionary War were in Braddock's army. Horatio Gates served as a junior officer in a British regiment. Nineteen-year-old Daniel Morgan drove a wagon carrying supplies. Both men became generals under Washington's command. Thomas Gage, who would become the head of the entire British Army in North America and was the Royal Governor of Massachusetts in 1775, also served in that campaign.

Braddock's defeat was a stunning disaster. It opened the Virginia and Pennsylvania frontiers to a series of deadly Indian raids. In that emergency Virginia commissioned 23-year-old George Washington to command a regiment to defend the frontier. For the next three years Washington served on the Virginia frontier.

Meanwhile, the major battles of the French and Indian War took place in the north. The British had the advantage of numbers. British settlers in North America outnumbered the French settlers in Canada 15 to 1. The British also had another advantage. Their Royal Navy warships controlled the waters along the Canadian

coast. The French had two advantages of their own. Their soldiers were better trained and more skilled at wilderness fighting. Most importantly, the French were much better at forming alliances with the Indians. By having the Indians on their side, the French could dominate wilderness fighting.

England sent reinforcements to North America. By 1758 the British were ready for a new campaign. British strategy had two parts. A land and sea force would try to control the St. Lawrence River. The river was the lifeline for New France. At the same time, a land force would advance against Lake Champlain in northern New York.

Because it was so hard to move an army through the American wilderness, armies tried to use rivers and lakes as natural highways. A canoe or boat could carry more supplies more easily than could a horse or ox

Battle of Lake George, 1755. Many men who became important American officers during the Revolution served in the British forces around Lake Champlain and in Canada. They included Ethan Allen, Benedict Arnold, and Israel Putnam.

In the spring of 1756 militia Captain Jeremiah Smith went to the western Virginia frontier to organize settlers to fight a raiding party of Indians. His group of 20 English settlers drove off a party of 50 Indians led by a French captain.

Above: The fortress of Louisbourg, in Nova Scotia, 1758. Strategists believed that whoever held Louisbourg controlled the sea lanes leading to Canada.

pulling a wagon along a primitive road. A series of streams and rivers fed into Lake Champlain and Lake George in New York. French forces could use that route to move south from Canada. British forces could use it to move north to attack Canada. Most of the important fighting took place around Lake Champlain. An especially valuable prize was Fort Ticonderoga, located on the southern end of Lake Champlain.

The first British attack against Fort Ticonderoga in 1758 was a disaster for the British. British and provincial forces received poor leadership from the British generals. Their attack against the fort suffered heavy losses. Many provincial officers were angry about the senseless, wasteful way the British generals used their men. The defeated British forces withdrew from Fort Ticonderoga. As time passed, England kept sending reinforcements from Europe to North America. The French could not match their numbers, so the British were able to keep trying. The next year they finally captured the fort.

While the fighting raged around Lake Champlain, the British prepared to attack the fortress of Louisbourg. Provincial forces had captured Louisbourg once before,

34

back in 1745. But by the terms of the peace treaty they had given it back to the French. During the summer of 1758 British forces landed near Louisbourg. They then marched inland and captured the fort again. The victory gave England control of the entrance to the St. Lawrence River. Control of the river meant that the British could attack the French capital at Quebec.

Finally the decisive battle of the French and Indian War came in 1759. A British army commanded by a very skilled general named James Wolfe sailed up the St. Lawrence River. It landed near Quebec and defeated the French on the Plains of Abraham just outside the city. During the battle both Wolfe and the French general, the Marquis de Montcalm, died. The next year the British completed the conquest of Canada. After France and England made a peace treaty, Canada became another British colony, just like the thirteen American colonies to the south.

The British victory in the French and Indian War ended the French threat to the colonies in North America. Americans and Britons shared the victory celebration. Neither realized that victory brought the American Revolution closer. The presence of France as a common enemy had been something that had held America and England together. The common enemy, France, had been like a glue connecting the provincials and the homeland. Now that glue was gone.

Left: Both England and France sent only a small part of their forces to fight in North America. For them the more important contest was for Europe, the West Indies, and India. The fighting between England and France spread to include many other European countries. In Europe the period of the French and Indian War is known as the Seven Years' War.

CHAPTER THREE

The Question of Taxes

*England spent an enormous amount of money to
defend the colonies from the Indians. How to pay for
it became a major conflict between the British
government and the Americans.*

The French and Indian War revealed some surprising
tensions between England and its American colonies.
From the British point of view the colonies had failed to
meet British requests for men, money, and supplies.
When American merchants did provide supplies, they
often charged outrageous prices. Worse yet, many
merchants continued to trade with the French even while
the war was going on. The British government and the
king believed that the provincials should be grateful for
all that the government had done for them. It angered
them when the Americans behaved otherwise.

The provincials did not see matters in the same light.
The British regulars had treated provincial soldiers as
second-class citizens. British officers had often insulted
everything American, from clothes to courage.
Many British officers had been too proud to
learn anything from the Americans. As a
result, provincial soldiers had died
needlessly. There were bad feelings on
both sides. But no one expected that
Americans would ever revolt against England. In 1760
Ben Franklin wrote that if the Americans "could not
agree to unite for their defense against the French and
Indians who are harassing their settlements, burning
their buildings and murdering their people, can it
reasonably be supposed there is any danger of their
uniting against their own nation, which protects and
encourages them, with which they have so many
connections and ties of blood, interest and affection."

The French surrender of Canada to the British gave the British control of all of the old French trading posts. When the British took over these posts, they treated the Indians with great self-importance, or arrogance. In that way they behaved differently from the French. The Indians did not care for the new behavior. What the Indians disliked even more was the fact that the British came as settlers instead of hunters, trappers, and traders. In 1763 many Indians began to attack the British. Fighting lasted for two years and was known as Pontiac's War, after the name of a great Indian leader.

There were two important results of Pontiac's War. In order to make peace with the Indians, the king decided that no Americans should be allowed to enter most of the lands west of the Allegheny Mountains. That meant that the colonies would not be allowed to expand. Pontiac's War also showed that the provincials needed the redcoats to protect them. The British government believed that the colonies needed about 10,000 soldiers. It cost about 350,000 pounds to maintain these British soldiers in North America. That was a heavy expense. It made perfect sense to the British that the Americans should have to pay part of the bill. After Pontiac's War the British government, or Parliament, decided that the provincials should help pay for the war's cost.

The Sugar Act

Up to the time of Pontiac's War Parliament had passed laws and put taxes on the colonies to control trade. But Parliament had never before set taxes on American citizens. Instead, the provincials had set their own taxes through the provincial legislatures. But in 1764 Parliament passed its first law with the specific goal of raising money in the colonies. That law was the Sugar Act. The colonies depended on trade carried by ships back and forth across the Atlantic to Europe. Trade with the West Indies was also very important. Ships left American ports carrying dried fish, lumber, naval stores, horses, and much more. They arrived in the French West Indies, the islands controlled by France, to trade these exports for molasses. The ships returned to America. There the imported molasses were processed into rum.

Above: The French and Indian War gave the provincials valuable military experience. Rogers Rangers, winter dress, 1758.

Opposite: All together, about 25,000 provincials served in the military during the French and Indian War. Rogers Rangers, summer dress, 1758.

The British naval commander in North America said in 1773 "that British Acts of Parliament will never go down in America, unless forced by the point of the sword." A modern replica of a British frigate enters the port of Boston.

Admiralty: England's department of the Navy; the office that enforces England's laws of the sea

Making and selling rum was a big business. The rum trade provided jobs, money, and the drink of choice for thousands of Americans. Almost all Americans who worked in that business avoided paying the taxes they were supposed to pay. They either smuggled the molasses and the rum in and out, or they paid the tax collectors a bribe, which was cheaper than paying the tax.

A tax on imports and exports is called a duty. The Sugar Act put many duties on American imports and exports. There were duties on refined sugar, coffee, indigo, iron, hides, and much more. The new duties greatly changed the rum trade. In the past, American merchants had ignored most duties. Many had even turned to smuggling, illegal import or export, to avoid duties. Parliament knew it had to do something to change that behavior. So it established new ways to enforce the Sugar Act.

The Royal Navy increased its patrols near American ports to prevent smuggling. The government appointed more customs commissioners, people who collected the duties on imports and exports. When British officials thought that a merchant had violated the laws on imports and exports, they sent him for trial. But the trial was not the usual type of civil trial with a jury. Instead, it was a trial in an **admiralty** court in distant Halifax, Nova Scotia. There was no jury there, and the merchant could be quite certain that he would be found guilty. Americans believed that trial in an admiralty court was

Above: Painters often made pictures showing the heroes of the Revolution. Many of these paintings exaggerated what took place. Compare this painting to the more realistic picture opposite.

taking away one of their most important freedoms, the freedom from false arrest.

The Stamp Act

In 1765 Parliament passed the Stamp Act to raise 60,000 more pounds to help cover the cost of supporting the soldiers. The Stamp Act was a tax on various types of printed material, including newspapers and legal documents. Some Americans agreed that the Stamp Act made sense. At first a handful of American leaders were quite happy to receive jobs as stamp agents to collect the new tax. In Virginia Richard Henry Lee applied to be a stamp agent. In Pennsylvania Benjamin Franklin tried to get the job for some of his friends. But the Stamp Act caused a storm that no one had expected.

Many Americans were already feeling uncomfortable about the Sugar Act. Then came a downturn in the economy, a depression. People are always more ready for change when the economy is poor. The Stamp Act made change happen quickly. It united Americans in every colony—printers, lawyers, merchants, ship

Above: A British tax stamp. There were one-penny stamps for newspapers and pamphlets, four-penny stamps for books, and more expensive stamps for more important documents. If lawyers or merchants tried to go ahead without the right stamps, they could be arrested. Then they would be tried in the admiralty courts.

Left: Patrick Henry concluded his speech to the Virginia House of Burgesses by reminding people, and the British King George III, about how tyrants were overthrown: "Caesar had his Brutus—Charles the first, his Cromwell—and George the third —may profit from their example.... If this be treason, make the most of it!"

owners—against the Stamp Act. They united behind the principle of *No Taxation without Representation*.

In New York City the arrival of the first stamps caused a riot. An anti-British mob controlled the streets. General Thomas Gage was the British commander-in-chief. He was in New York when the riot occurred. He ordered his soldiers to man the fort but told them not to fire except in self-defense. He then waited until the mobs went home. The experience taught Gage a lesson. The best way to deal with American anger was to wait until the Americans calmed down.

But many Americans did not calm down. In Virginia 29-year-old Patrick Henry gave a fiery speech to the colonial government, the House of Burgesses. It became known as his treason speech. The legislators toned down Henry's speech. On May 31, 1765, they adopted the Virginia Resolves. The resolves said that the local government would continue to make its own laws for Virginia. It also declared that taxation without

Opposite: A mob wrecks the home of Thomas Hutchinson, the chief justice who tried to enforce the Stamp Act, during the riots of 1765.

burgess: a citizen of a burg or borough; used here to mean a representative to the lower house of the Maryland or Virginia colonial legislature, called House of Burgesses

Below: British cartoonists took aim at current events with their sharpened pens. One marked the repeal of the Stamp Act with a cartoon of its "funeral."

representation was illegal. Rhode Island quickly announced its support for the Virginia Resolves. Around the same time in Charleston, South Carolina, political leaders said: It is "essential to the freedom of a people and the undoubted rights of Englishmen that no taxes be imposed upon them but by their own consent."

Everywhere the opponents of the Stamp Act moved quickly. In 1765 they formed the Sons of Liberty. The Sons of Liberty called themselves "Patriots." They gathered in mobs to frighten the stamp agents. Samuel Adams led one Boston group. On August 26, 1765, they burned court records, looted the home of a British tax official, and wrecked the home of the chief justice who enforced the laws. In other places the Sons of Liberty tarred and feathered British officials. The campaign of fear begun by the Sons of Liberty worked. All the stamp agents resigned before the Stamp Act even became the official law.

James Otis was the foremost lawyer in Massachusetts. He had given up a profitable job rather than support British restrictions on American trade. Otis began a movement that led to the Stamp Act Congress. It brought together leaders from eight of the colonies. They met from October 7 to 25 in New York City. The Stamp Act Congress was more moderate than the Sons of Liberty. That congress concluded with a Declaration of Rights and Grievances. It denied Parliament's right to tax the colonies.

Benjamin Franklin had changed his mind. He was on official business in London and spoke to the House of Commons. He said that the colonies should not pay the stamp tax. He warned that if British soldiers tried to enforce the Stamp Act, it might cause rebellion. At the same time, British merchants wanted to end the Stamp Act because it was hurting trade with the American colonies.

Pressure from British merchants, Franklin, and others convinced Parliament to repeal, or cancel, the Stamp Act. On March 18, 1766, King George III accepted the decision. When the news reached America, people rejoiced. It seemed that the biggest troubles were over. Most people agreed with the leader who said, "Let the past, like the falling out of lovers, prove only the renewal of love."

CHAPTER FOUR

The Breach Widens

The dispute over the Stamp Act showed that the real question was, "What were the rights of King and Parliament, and what were the rights of the colonists?"

Most Americans did not realize that at the same time King George III had accepted the repeal of the Stamp Act, he had made another decision. That decision became the Declaratory Act. The Declaratory Act stated Parliament's right to make laws for the colonies in "every point of legislation whatsoever." At the same time Parliament was reminding American leaders that it made the laws, many Americans were saying that they should make their own laws. King George and most British leaders believed that the Americans needed to be taught a lesson. So Parliament imposed a new set of taxes, the Townsend Revenue Act of 1767. The Townsend Revenue Act set duties on glass, lead, painters' colors, imported paper, and tea. Like the Stamp Act, it was meant to help pay for the military defense of the colonies. Like the Stamp Act, the Townsend Revenue Act produced fierce opposition from the Americans.

Some of the opposition turned violent. There were riots at various ports. The Sons of Liberty attacked customs agents. At the same time, American political leaders loudly criticized the royal governors. The American leaders decided to hit back at England by limiting British imports into the colonies. This type of economic effort is known as a nonimportation agreement or boycott. By boycotting British imports, American leaders hoped to pressure the British government to repeal the Townsend Act.

Toward the end of September 1768 a large number of ships appeared in Boston harbor. They carried three

regiments of red-coated British regulars. Their job was to act like a police force and protect the tax collectors. The redcoats needed shelter. By a law called the Quartering Act the colonies were supposed to provide shelter, or quarters, to the king's army. The people of Boston claimed that there were no quarters available. So the British commander took over public buildings, including the State House itself.

The soldiers and the Bostonians did not get along. There were frequent fistfights between soldiers who were off duty and local citizens. Neither side made efforts to get along. Bostonians urged the soldiers to desert. British officers, in turn, took special delight in bothering public leaders. Tension built toward the evening of March 5, 1770.

A gang of Boston toughs began throwing sticks and snowballs at a redcoat guard near the Customs House. A small unit of redcoats came to the guard's support. But the gang surrounded them and pushed closer. A British captain rushed to the scene. What exactly happened next is not clear. The captain probably shouted to his men, "not to Fire, not to Fire, not to Fire." Perhaps some nervous soldier only heard the

Not only did painters exaggerate the heroes of the Revolution, they also exaggerated the events. This heroic representation of the Boston Massacre hangs in the Capitol building in Washington, D.C.

word "Fire." Without a doubt a soldier squeezed his musket's trigger and fired his weapon. Several other soldiers also fired. By the time the smoke cleared, three citizens lay dead, and two received mortal wounds. That was the so-called "Boston Massacre."

Royal Governor Hutchinson ordered a trial of the British soldiers involved in the firing. Two Massachusetts lawyers, John Adams and Josiah Quincy, bravely stepped forward to defend the soldiers. They knew that it would make them unpopular with many Americans. The court decided that most of the soldiers were not guilty. The court said two soldiers were guilty of manslaughter. They received the punishment of being branded, having their hands burned by a piece of hot iron. The patriot leader, Samuel Adams, was unhappy with the result. He and his **radical** allies kept up the pressure. One of the most important tools used by the radicals was the Committees of Correspondence.

The Sons of Liberty created the Committees of Correspondence in 1772. The goal was to help patriots throughout the colonies to work together. The committees exchanged news and opinions by corresponding, or writing letters. The committees planned how to change public opinion so that more and more people would turn against British rule. Samuel Adams organized the first Committee of Correspondence in Boston. Patrick Henry and Thomas Jefferson worked to create a committee in Virginia.

Skillful patriotic writers and members of the Committees of Correspondence turned the so-called Boston Massacre into a major piece of news. In Boston Paul Revere made an engraving, a type of picture made by cutting or carving into metal or wood, that claimed to show what had taken place. In fact, it was a false picture. Other radicals also made false claims that stirred up American citizens everywhere. The Committees of Correspondence spread the news. They knew that the image of unarmed American citizens shot to death by British soldiers would be a powerful tool. Their efforts worked. The Boston Massacre turned many people against British rule.

As time passed, the strategy of boycotting British goods also began to work. All of the colonies except

radical: extreme; in favor of rapid or violent social change; refers to either a point of view or the person who holds that point of view

New Hampshire joined in the boycott. Between 1768 and 1769 the value of British imports went down by almost 40 percent. Parliament repealed most of the Townsend Revenue Act in 1770. Only the duty on tea remained. The success of the boycott gave confidence to those Americans who wanted more freedom from England. It also angered King George and many British

Crispus Attucks, a former slave, was a leader of the gang that started the confrontation. He was one of the men killed by British gunfire.

officials. They worried that if America successfully resisted taxation, what might happen elsewhere? Perhaps Ireland would try to evade its taxes. Perhaps all of England might break up. That fear haunted King George and influenced all of his decisions. He believed that he had to be tough with America to keep the British Empire from falling apart.

The conflict between the American colonies and the Crown produced something new in British politics. Some British politicians linked the American demands for liberty with calls for more liberty in England itself. They saw the king as a tyrant. They began a tremendous political attack against the government and the king. They were friends to America. One defender of American rights was Edmund Burke. Burke was a brilliant speaker. He described how the colonists came from Great Britain. He continued by noting that the

This picture of the Boston Massacre comes closer to the truth than any of the others in this book. The British soldiers appear to be surrounded, and only some of them are firing into the crowd.

American colonists had to be fierce and independent to survive in North America. Burke concluded that because the Americans were fierce, because they were independent, and most importantly because they had "sprung from a nation [England] in whose veins the blood of freedom circulates," they especially cherished their freedom. Burke said that it would be a mistake to try to change them.

In summary, the political debate in England caused British attitudes to harden. A minority were friends of America. A majority were against the Americans. The king did not change his mind. He still wanted to teach the Americans a lesson. He believed that the duty on tea must be kept as a symbol of his control over the American colonies. The Americans responded by boycotting legal tea and smuggling illegal tea.

The Royal Navy had the duty of patrolling the American coast to prevent smuggling. The coast from Maine to Florida is long and full of places where smugglers can operate, so the Royal Navy was stretched very thin. There were many shallow bays and coves where large warships could not sail. Smaller British ships patrolled those places. One of the patrols was a schooner called the *Gaspée*. On the night of June 9, 1772, the *Gaspée* was chasing a ship in Narragansett Bay, Rhode

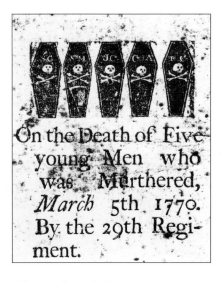

Above: Broadsides, or posters, were a common means for patriots to publicize their ideas about current events. This broadside shows outrage at the deaths in Boston.

Below: The attack on the British patrol ship *Gaspée* as it founders off the coast of Rhode Island. The British government called this act a crime of high treason.

Island. Suddenly the *Gaspée* ran aground. A Rhode Island sailor named Abraham Whipple led a group to attack the helpless *Gaspée*. Whipple and his men burned the British ship and then escaped. The burning of the *Gaspée* was a violent challenge to British rule.

The British prime minister at that difficult time was Frederick North. North worked closely with King George. The two men got along very well. North received advice from a seven-man cabinet, but he made all important decisions himself. He could depend on solid support from the House of Lords. He had to be more careful with the House of Commons. Still, even

A 1770 broadside advising patriots to boycott a Boston merchant who imported goods from England. British exports to America fell some 40 percent because of the boycott.

there a large majority supported his decisions because all members of parliament knew that the king supported North. North had already confronted difficult problems in other parts of the British empire. He had dealt firmly with problems in Ireland and India. That gave him confidence that he could do the same with America.

So North responded firmly to the *Gaspée* affair. He created a Commission of Inquiry with power to send suspects to Britain for trial. British officials offered a large reward for information about who had attacked the *Gaspée*. No one could uncover enough evidence to try Whipple and his men for the crime. Instead, some New Englanders, particularly sailors, merchants, and smugglers, celebrated the destruction of the *Gaspée*. British officials and most people in England saw it differently. To them it was another example of increasing lawlessness, or mob law, in America.

In 1773 North made another fateful decision. It had to do with the East India Company and tea. The East India Company was a powerful British trading

William Tryon already had experience in using troops to keep the peace. He had been the royal governor of North Carolina before he came to New York. While he was there, he restored order several times by leading troops against the Regulators, a group that violently opposed royal authority. Until Tryon finally defeated the Regulators in 1771, they gathered in huge mobs to disrupt the local government and run people out of town.

company. In 1773 it was having money trouble. North decided to help the company. So Parliament made the East India Company the only company that could legally sell tea in the colonies. The East India Company set its price below the price of smuggled tea. The idea was that Americans would buy East India tea since that tea was the cheapest.

Most of the tea merchants in New York and Philadelphia sold smuggled tea. They worried that they would lose their business to the East India Company. These merchants began a campaign against the East India Company. They pointed out that the East India tea still carried the hated tea tax. They said that making the East India tea cheap was a trick to get Americans to pay the tax. They also said that the Tea Act raised a frightening question: If Parliament could control the tea trade, what might it do next? Parliament might try to take over all American trade.

The campaign worked by changing attitudes. One patriot told his fellow countrymen, "Do not suffer yourself to sip the accursed, dutied stuff. For if you do, the devil will immediately enter into you, and you will instantly become a traitor to your country." American

Americans attended meetings to plan how they would prevent the landing of British tea.

50

patriots decided to boycott the East India tea. Others took more dramatic action.

Seven hundred people met in Philadelphia in October 1773. They decided to put pressure on the eight men who had the right to sell East India tea. Groups of bullies threatened these men. They scared them into quitting their jobs. Only one tea seller remained, and he was aboard the tea ship *Polly* that was due to arrive in Philadelphia soon. So the mob spread the threat that any pilot who brought the *Polly* into Philadelphia would be tarred and feathered.

The Americans tried the same thing in New York City. However, there the royal governor, William Tryon, had soldiers to keep the peace. Tryon was pretty certain that the soldiers could protect the tea ship that was sailing to New York. Tryon may have been right, but he failed to think what else the Americans might do. The merchant-smugglers did what had been done in Philadelphia. They organized a mob to visit the tea sellers and threaten them. They even published a handbill, or poster, that threatened "an unwelcome visit" to anyone who helped the East India Company. Before a tea ship arrived in New York, all of the tea sellers had been driven from their jobs.

History best remembers what took place in Boston. But the events in Philadelphia and New York happened first. Patriots in both ports took steps to block the tea before it arrived.

Samuel Adams graduated from Harvard and squandered his family's fortune before he rose to fame as a radical politician. Samuel Adams' energy helped start the Revolution. He was less useful in later years when the Continental Congress had to make practical decisions.

The Famous Tea Party

In December 1773 three East India Company ships arrived in Boston harbor with their cargoes of tea. Unlike the other ports, Boston had often imported taxed tea. Boston patriots thought that it was shameful. So they decided to do something different. The Committee of Correspondence knew that the tea was coming, so they were ready when the tea ships arrived. Boston toughs had already forced the tea sellers to flee for safety. Now they prevented the tea from being unloaded. Then Samuel Adams stepped forward. Adams believed in direct action to arouse Americans against England.

That belief made Adams and men like him radicals. The radicals were a minority. Many more Americans were still loyal to the Crown or did not have strong political views one way or the other. However, Adams had important backing from American merchants who made a lot of money by smuggling tea.

Samuel Adams organized a group to attack the ships. On the evening of December 16, 1773, a 150-man mob dressed up as Mohawk Indians. They wore the costumes to disguise themselves. Then they boarded the ships and threw 342 chests of tea overboard. The incident became known as "the Boston Tea Party." The disguises fooled no one. Everyone knew who had carried out the Boston Tea Party.

The local newspaper, the Boston Gazette, proudly reported:

"A number of resolute men (dressed like Mohawks or Indians) determined to do all in their power to save their country from the ruin which their enemies had plotted, in less than four hours emptied every chest of tea on board the three ships...into the sea.... The people are almost [all] congratulating each other on this happy event."

Paul Revere carried the news to the members of the New York Committee of Correspondence. A member wrote back to Samuel Adams, "Before the arrival...of the news from Boston, the Citizens of New York had got to be divided.... But immediately they became united and determined that [the tea] should not be landed." The unity of the New Yorkers persuaded Governor Tryon that the situation was hopeless. When New York's tea ship arrived, he told it to turn around and go back home with its load of tea.

News of the Boston Tea Party reached Philadelphia on the very day the tea ship *Polly* appeared. A mass meeting of patriots gathered and made their feelings clear. The tea ship returned home rather than face the mob. Charleston, South Carolina, was the fourth great American port. Like Boston, it had a history of importing legal tea and paying the duty. Because it was so far from Boston, Charleston's people did not know about the Boston Tea Party at the time the tea ship *London* arrived. But local politicians knew about the growing protest against tea in the other colonies. At first they arranged a public meeting. People voted to send the *London* home. But the royal governor of South Carolina managed to land the tea anyway. So the patriots in Charleston did the same thing that the Sons of Liberty had done in the other ports. They frightened the tea sellers and kept the unloaded tea from being sold.

The Boston Tea Party marked the beginning of violence in the dispute over taxes. Because of the Boston Tea Party the American colonies moved from resistance to revolution. The Sons of Liberty, the radicals, seemed to have taken control. That frightened many people. A group of 100 Boston merchants offered to pay for the damage done to the company that owned the tea, the East India Company. Benjamin Franklin also thought it was the right thing to do. But the radicals blocked the repayment.

The actions in Boston and the other American ports horrified many people in England. To them it seemed

In the days before photography was invented, every artist could present a different version of important events like the Boston Tea Party.

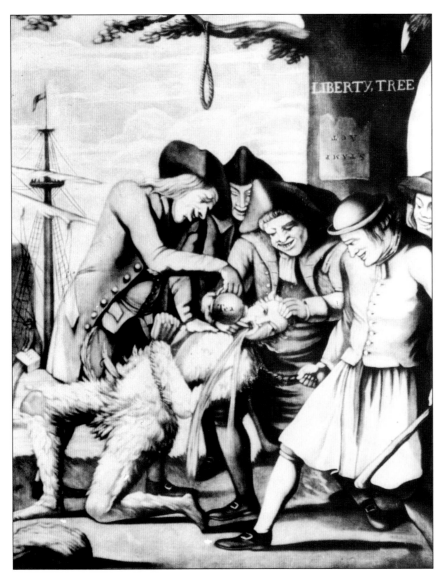

At the port of Falmouth, Massachusetts, the Sons of Liberty tarred and feathered a customs officer named John Malcolm. Malcolm fled to Boston. On the night of January 25, 1774, a mob took Malcolm from his house in Boston. Again they tarred and feathered him. The mob dragged Malcolm around town while beating and whipping him. They forced him to drink large quantities of tea and threatened to hang him at Boston's Liberty Tree. This British cartoon shows Malcolm choking on the tea.

Political cartoons explored the difficult issues of the day. One patriot shared the problem facing all Americans: "I cannot think myself a rebel, or a traitor. I love my King, revere the Parliament, and have the highest . . . regard for the mother country." But he warned that if British officials thought that the colonies would let Massachusetts struggle alone, they were wrong.

that America was controlled by a violent mob of radicals. Just as the Sugar Act and Stamp Act had united Americans against British authority, so the Boston Tea Party united Englishmen against the Americans. So Parliament cracked down on what seemed to be the main source of the trouble, Boston. It would make Boston an example to teach all the colonies a lesson.

Parliament passed the Boston Port Act, which went into effect on June 1, 1774. It closed the port until damages were paid for the destruction of the tea. Parliament also decided to place Massachusetts under strict military control. The office of royal governor went to a military man, General Thomas Gage. Parliament also passed a law giving the Massachusetts royal governor control over the town meetings. The people of Massachusetts cherished their town meetings. They were where they settled many local conflicts. They were central to their idea of liberty, and now could not be held unless General Gage gave written approval. Parliament added some other laws to protect royal officials who worked collecting the taxes. It renewed an old law called the Quartering Act. The Quartering Act forced the people of Boston to open their houses to British soldiers to provide them with shelter, or quarters.

The Boston Port Act was not the only act that united the colonies. Long before the Boston Tea Party Parliament had been thinking about what to do with Canada. Shortly after it passed the Boston Port Act, Parliament also passed the Quebec Act. That act gave the province of Canada control of most territory west of the Allegheny Mountains. Another law forbade Americans from settling west of the mountains. Because

Nobody welcomed the knock of a British soldier once Parliament passed the Quartering Act.

British Reactions to the Boston Tea Party

"I am much hurt that the [behavior] of bad men hath drawn the people of Boston to take such unjustifiable steps; but I trust by degrees tea will find its way there."
King George III, December 19, 1774

"The dispute with America is now become more serious than ever. It is reduced to the decisive question, whether the right of taxation be here or there. There is no medium [compromise] which can be adopted with honour or safety on either side . . . the opposition in America is not to the sum levied [duties and taxes] but to the right of levying [taxing] it."
London Evening Post, January 27, 1774

"I very much fear the question . . . will be nothing less than whether the colonies of America are, or not, the colonies of England . . . we [England] cannot subsist [survive] without the advantages from our commerce in America. Those advantages can never be maintained if we [do not] keep up the sovereign authority of this country." George Rice, Member of Parliament, March 1774

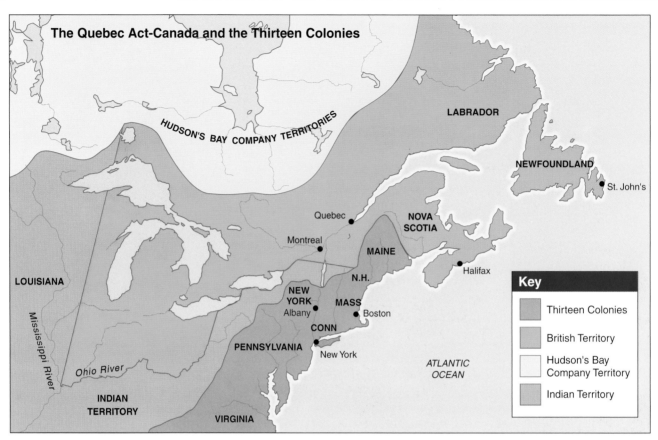

The Quebec Act-Canada and the Thirteen Colonies

HUDSON'S BAY COMPANY TERRITORIES

LABRADOR

NEWFOUNDLAND

St. John's

LOUISIANA

Quebec

NOVA SCOTIA

Montreal

MAINE

N.H.

Halifax

NEW YORK

MASS

Albany

Boston

CONN

Mississippi River

Ohio River

PENNSYLVANIA

New York

ATLANTIC OCEAN

INDIAN TERRITORY

VIRGINIA

Key

Thirteen Colonies

British Territory

Hudson's Bay Company Territory

Indian Territory

of the Quebec Act, New Englanders feared the spread of French-speaking Catholics from Canada into the western territories. Also because of the Quebec Act Virginians lost the chance to buy and sell land in the Ohio River valley. Wealthy New Englanders and Virginians had always mistrusted one another. Then they found common cause in their opposition to the Quebec Act. Since so many of the leaders of the Revolutionary War came from Massachusetts and Virginia, that proved very important.

Americans called Parliament's set of laws "the Intolerable Acts." They were serious blows to the American economy and to political freedom. Even more so than had been the case with the Stamp Act, the Intolerable Acts united American patriots.

Long after the Revolutionary War John Adams looked back. He remarked, "The Revolution was effected before the war commenced. The Revolution was in the minds and hearts of the people. . . . This radical change in the principles, opinions, sentiments, and affections of the people was the real American Revolution."

Opposite: British cartoon, published in London in 1774, showing residents of Boston "caged" by the Boston Port Act.

CHAPTER FIVE

The Resistance Spreads

American patriots responded to the Intolerable Acts by organizing the First Continental Congress.

Three days after Boston learned about the Boston Port Act, Sam Adams led a meeting. His group passed a resolution and sent it to the other colonies:

"...It is the opinion of this town [Boston], that if the other colonies came into a joint resolution to stop all importations from England, and exportations to England, and every port of the West Indies, till the Act for blocking up this harbour be repealed, [it] will prove the salvation of North America and her Liberties."

Even in Boston, merchants disagreed. One hundred twenty-three merchants sent a letter to the king saying they did not support the Tea Party. A large number of merchants decided that instead of supporting the boycott, they would move their business to other ports in Massachusetts. Radicals belonging to Boston's Committee of Correspondence took steps to stop them.

Next, Paul Revere carried the news of the Boston Port Act all of the way to Philadelphia. He returned with good news for the Boston Committee of Correspondence. Neither the great port of Philadelphia nor New York would

Carpenters' Hall, Philadelphia, the meeting place of the First Continental Congress in 1774.

take advantage of Boston being closed. Instead, they would support Boston. The other twelve colonies rallied only partially to Massachusetts. They did not support Sam Adams' call for a boycott. Instead, they called for a Continental Congress.

Virginia led the way. Virginians in the House of Burgesses remembered the success of the Stamp Act Congress. They responded to the Intolerable Acts by passing a resolution that "A Congress should be appointed . . . from all the Colonies" to make a plan "for the defense and preservation of our common rights." All of the colonies except Georgia agreed. Georgia was the least settled of the colonies. It was a frontier colony that needed money from England so it could grow. Georgia also faced more Indian attacks than the other colonies. It needed England to defend it. So Georgia was not yet ready to challenge the king.

The First Continental Congress met in Philadelphia in September 1774. In Carpenters' Hall delegates argued and debated. The delegates represented many positions and came from different ways of life. There were merchants and farmers, large and small land owners, cautious men and radicals, northerners and southerners. Slowly the delegates began to work together. Patrick Henry said with great emotion, "The distinctions between Virginians, Pennsylvanians, New Yorkers, and New Englanders are no more. I am not a Virginian, but an American!"

One day Paul Revere rode into Philadelphia carrying dramatic news. He reported that there had been a meeting in Suffolk County, Massachusetts. There men had written a statement known as "the Suffolk Resolves." The president of the Congress, Peyton Randolph, read them aloud. The Suffolk Resolves stated that the Intolerable Acts were unconstitutional, not

Not everyone agreed with the actions of the First Continental Congress [below]. A New York farmer protested that the Congress had "taken no one step that tended to peace: they have gone from bad to worse, and have either ignorantly misunderstood, carelessly neglected, or basely betrayed the interests of all the Colonies."

according to the law, so they should not be obeyed. The Suffolk Resolves urged people to form a government of their own. They should collect their own taxes and not give them to royal authorities until Parliament repealed the Intolerable Acts. Meanwhile, Massachusetts should gather arms and form its own militia.

Delegates exploded with shouts and cheers. They gathered around the Massachusetts delegates to congratulate them. The First Continental Congress adopted the Suffolk Resolves without a change. It seemed that the radicals had convinced most delegates that dramatic action was needed. Still, almost everyone agreed with John Adams, who said, "There is not a man among us that would not be happy to see accommodation with Britain." Another delegate cried, "Independence? A hundred times no!"

The First Continental Congress concluded with a set of resolutions. They plainly set forth the rights to life, liberty, property, and the rights of assemblies (the local colonial governments) to tax and make local laws. These words moved the quarrel with England beyond just taxes. The conflict became both taxes and whether Parliament had the right to make laws for America. To put force behind the words, the Congress decided that as of December 1, 1774, all imports from England were to end. To make it work, the Congress formed a Continental Association. A committee was to be elected in every village, town, and city to enforce the decrees made by the Continental Association. All of the colonies except New York and Georgia joined the Association.

The delegates finished their business by agreeing to meet again in May 1775 if the king and Parliament did not change the Intolerable Acts. Then the delegates left Philadelphia. They had boldly issued a defiant call aimed at royal authority. In the past patriot leaders had challenged successfully the king and Parliament and without bloodshed. They expected the same result again.

The delegates did not know what King George was saying at that time. If they had, the delegates would have seen that economic pressure would not work. On

King George III. Before he knew the results of the First Continental Congress, he told Prime Minister North: "The die is now cast. The colonies must either submit or triumph. I do not wish to come to severer measures but we must not retreat."

November 18 the king wrote to Prime Minister North to say, "... The New England governments are in a state of rebellion; blows must decide whether they are to be subject to this country or independent."

Meanwhile, General Gage returned to Boston to act both as royal governor of Massachusetts and commander-in-chief of the British army in America. Before he left England, he told King George that as long as the British government acted like "lambs," the Americans would act like "lions." But if the British government acted firmly, the Americans would act like

Right: General Thomas Gage was in London when he heard news about the Boston Tea Party. He noted, "People talk more seriously than ever about America: that the crisis is come, when the provinces must be either British colonies, or independent and separate states."

Below: A story was told about British soldiers harassing some Boston schoolboys by repeatedly breaking the ice in their skating pond and knocking down the hills they built in the snow. The boys finally went to General Gage and "demanded satisfaction." Gage was said to have been so impressed with their courage that he made sure his soldiers never bothered them again. An artist depicted this story in 1875 to commemorate the centennial of the Revolution.

lambs. King George liked that sort of talk. He thought that Gage would quickly restore order in Boston.

When Gage arrived in Boston, he found that things were not as simple as they had seemed when looked at from far-away London. England only controlled the places where it had soldiers. Outside of Boston the radicals were in control. They held illegal meetings to organize resistance to British rule. They prevented the work of the courts of law. Gage became worried. He ordered the army's supply of ammunition moved from Cambridge, a town outside of Boston, to Boston itself. When soldiers marched to carry out the order, armed mobs gathered. There was no violence, but the affair should have warned Gage about what could happen when soldiers went into the countryside.

The winter of 1774-75 was difficult for the British soldiers in Boston. At every turn it seemed that Bostonians were doing something to annoy the redcoats. When British officers knocked on doors to ask for quarters, they were told the house was full. When General Gage gave orders for his soldiers to build their own quarters, the soldiers found that Boston had no bricks to sell. When Gage offered high pay to Bostonians so they would build quarters for his soldiers, the laborers

Above: Tories in Boston lived in fear of attack. An angry mob might seize their chosen victim from his home and run him out of town.

refused to work. Gage's spies told him that resistance to England was spreading. Gage reported that Americans everywhere were taking up arms against the king. He said that they were "not a Boston rabble but the freeholders [people who owned property] and farmers of the country." In other words, the problem was no longer just the radicals and their gangs of bullies. Respectable men were joining the militia.

Gage kept trying to get along with the provincials. But he also prepared for conflict. He recalled British garrisons from distant places to Boston. Soon redcoats packed the city. Many British officers sensed that the situation was getting worse. At the end of January 1775 a British lieutenant wrote in his diary that the provincials were "making every preparation for resistance. They are taking every means to provide themselves with Arms." Whenever a British force marched from Boston, men on horseback followed at a safe distance. Clearly they were spying on the soldiers.

People still loyal to King George, the loyalists or Tories, became fearful. One of them was named Timothy Ruggles. What happened to him is an example of how patriots bullied the loyalists. Ruggles was a veteran of the French and Indian War. He was known to be brave, and he was known to be loyal to the king. He lived in a town outside of Boston. His neighbors included men who belonged to the Sons of Liberty and men who belonged to the militia. They did not like Ruggles and his talk about support for the king. So they decided to scare him away. They poisoned his cattle. They crept into his barn and painted his favorite horse with ugly colors. That gesture was a warning. It was meant to say, "What we can do to your horse, we can do to you and your family."

Although he was brave, Ruggles could not stand up to this. He joined the hundreds of loyalists who flocked to Boston where the king's soldiers and the Royal Navy could provide safety. There were many extra mouths to feed. Yet patriots refused to sell food to the redcoats and Tories. They had to depend on food brought by ship to Boston. Winter weather made food delivery uncertain. All that General Gage could do was hope that things would get better in the spring.

Below: In England people believed that events were out of control in America, like runaway horses dragging a carriage over a cliff to certain destruction.

Chronology

1607: A group of Englishmen land on the coast of Virginia. The settlement they establish becomes Jamestown, the first settlement to survive.

February 22, 1732: George Washington is born in Virginia.

1754: Lieutenant-Colonel George Washington, age 22, of the Virginia militia, fights the French and Indians in western Pennsylvania. The battles mark the beginning of the French and Indian War in North America, which leads to the Seven Years' War in Europe.

1754 to 1763: The French and Indian War takes place.

1756 to 1763: The Seven Years' War is fought in Europe.

1760: George III becomes king of England at the age of 22.

1764: England's Parliament passes the Sugar Act, which requires American colonists to pay England import and export taxes on a variety of goods, including sugar.

1765: England passes the Stamp Act, which requires Americans to pay taxes on many printed documents, including newspapers and legal documents.

1766: Reacting to American opposition, England repeals the Stamp Act.

1767: England imposes a new set of taxes on the American colonies, called the Townsend Revenue Act.

Americans react with widespread rioting and boycotts of British goods.

1768: England sends troops to Boston to enforce the laws and protect tax collectors. They use the Quartering Act to take over buildings for housing the soldiers.

March 5, 1770: A gang of Americans throws rocks at British soldiers, one of whom fires his musket. The so-called "Boston Massacre" takes place, leaving five colonists dead.

1770: England repeals most taxes, except the one on tea.

December 16, 1773: The most famous of several tea-related protests occurs. It is known as the Boston Tea Party. A gang of Bostonians, disguised as Indians, boards three ships and throws hundreds of cases of tea overboard.

June 1, 1774: To punish the people of Boston for the Boston Tea Party, and to regain control of the colony, England passes a set of laws that close down the port of Boston and put the city under martial law, or military rule. The Americans call the laws the Intolerable Acts.

September 1774: In response to the Intolerable Acts the First Continental Congress meets in Philadelphia. The Congress shows its defiance of British rule by stating that only the local colonial legislatures have the right to make laws for the colonies.

Glossary

ADMIRALTY: England's department of the navy; the office that enforces England's laws of the sea

ALLIANCE: an agreement between two or more nations to fight on the same side in any conflict

AMBUSH: a surprise attack launched from a hiding place

AMERICA: usually refers to the United States of America, but really means the land that contains the continents of North America, and South America

ARTILLERY: a group of cannons and other large guns used to help an army by firing at enemy troops

BOYCOTT: an organized effort to refuse to buy from or sell to a particular person or business

BRIBE: an illegal secret payment given to an official in return for an unfair favor

BRITISH: the nationality of a person born in Great Britain (England, Scotland, Wales, Northern Ireland); someone from England is called English

BURGESS: a citizen of a burg or borough; used here to mean a representative to the lower house of the Maryland or Virginia colonial legislature, called House of Burgesses

CASH CROP: a crop grown to sell for cash, such as tobacco; as opposed to a crop grown for one's own use, such as vegetables

CASUALTIES: people wounded, killed, or missing after a battle

CHARTER: document containing rules for running an organization or government

CIVIL WAR: a war between two groups in the same country

COLONY: a land that is owned and controlled by a particular nation, but is not really a part of that nation; a colonist is a permanent settler of a colony, as opposed to a temporary official sent by the "mother" country that controls the colony

COMMANDER-IN-CHIEF: an official who is the top controller, or officer, of a country's military forces

COMMISSION: (1) orders that make a person a military officer; (2) a group of officials assigned to do a specific job

CONGRESS: a group of people representing the general population for the purpose of making decisions

CONTINENTAL: an inhabitant of a continent; in this book an inhabitant of the thirteen colonies in the continent of North America

CROSSBELT: a belt that runs from the front of a waist belt over one shoulder to the back of the waist belt; a feature of military uniforms

CROWN: when capitalized, refers to a king or queen at the head of a nation

CUSTOMS: the government office that controls all things brought into a country, usually by charging a tax, or duty

DELEGATE: a representative sent to a congress, meeting, or convention

DEMOCRACY: government by the people; majority rule

DESERTER: a soldier or sailor who leaves the army or navy without permission

DUTY: a tax charged on goods brought into a country

EMPIRE: all of the colonies controlled by a particular nation

EXPORT/IMPORT: an export is an item sent out of one's own country to be sold to people in a foreign country; an import is an item produced in a foreign country and sent to one's home country

FORMATION: soldiers arranged in a certain order for marching or battle

FRENCH AND INDIAN WAR: a war fought in North America between the British and the French for control of the land west of the Allegheny Mountains. It was called the French and Indian War because the French recruited American Indians to fight with them.

GARRISON: fort or military post; the group of soldiers stationed at a fort

INDIANS: the name given to all Native Americans at the time Europeans settled the New World

LEGISLATURE: the group of government officials, usually elected, that makes the laws of a nation

LOYALIST: an American colonist who wanted America to remain part of the British empire

MILITIA: a group of citizens not normally part of the army who organize for the purpose of defending their homeland in an emergency; also used as a plural to describe several such groups

MODERATE: not extreme or radical; refers either to a point of view or to a person who holds that point of view

MONARCH/MONARCHY: a king or queen who rules a nation, usually by inheriting the position; a nation ruled by a monarch is a monarchy

MORTAL WOUND: a wound that eventually causes death

MUSKET: the forerunner to the rifle, used by foot soldiers in battle. Muskets were not as accurate as rifles

NAVAL STORES: products used to maintain ships; turpentine, resin, tar, and pitch

NEW NORLD/OLD WORLD: the New World is the western hemisphere, including North, Central, and South America; the Old World refers to Europe, Asia, and Africa, so called because people in the eastern part of the world did not know the western hemisphere existed until the fifteenth century

PARLIAMENT: the legislature of Great Britain

PATRIOT: an American who wanted the colonies to be independent of the British Empire; from patriotic, which means devoted to the good of one's country

PLANTER: the owner of a plantation

POUNDS: the currency, or form of money, used by the British

PRIME MINISTER: the chief executive of the British government

PROVINCE/PROVINCIAL: a colony; a territory controlled by a distant nation; a person who lives in a province is a provincial

RADICAL: extreme; in favor of rapid or violent social change; refers to either a point of view or the person who holds that point of view

REDCOATS: British soldiers, who typically wore a uniform with a red coat

REGIMENT: a military organization made up of companies

REGULARS: professional soldiers who belong to the army full time

REINFORCEMENTS: soldiers sent into a battle, after it has begun, to help their side win

REPEAL: cancel, undo

ROYAL GOVERNOR: a governor appointed by a monarch to run a colony

SEVEN YEARS' WAR: a war for control of central Europe that lasted from 1756 to 1763. Austria, France, Russia, Sweden, and Saxony joined together to destroy Prussia, and England took Prussia's side. The war consisted of land battles in Europe, widespread sea battles, and the French and Indian War in North America.

SKIRMISH: a brief battle involving a small number of soldiers; often part of a larger battle

SMUGGLING: importing goods without paying the required duties, or importing forbidden goods

STRATEGY: the overall plan for organizing troops to fight a battle or war

SUBJECTS: people who are under the power of a monarch

TARRED AND FEATHERED: in colonial times, a mob that disapproved of somebody's actions would humiliate their victims by covering them with tar and feathers, which were extremely hard to remove

TAX: a payment required by a government, usually a portion of money earned

TORY: someone who sided with Great Britain during the American Revolution; taken from the name of a political party in England

TRAITOR: someone who betrays their country by trying to harm it

TREASON: the crime of betraying one's country

TYRANT: a cruel ruler who has complete power over his subjects

WEST INDIES: the islands of the Caribbean Sea, so called because they were once thought to be a part of India

WORLD WAR: a war involving a large number of nations in different parts of the world

Further Resources

Books:

Carter, Alden R. *Colonies in Revolt.* New York: Franklin Watts, 1988.

Collier, Christopher and James Lincoln Collier. *The American Revolution, 1763-1783.* Tarrytown, NY: Marshall Cavendish Corp., 1998.

Collier, Christopher and James Lincoln Collier. *The French and Indian War, 1660-1763.* Tarrytown, NY: Marshall Cavendish Corp., 1998.

Denenberg, Barry. *The Journal of William Thomas Emerson: A Revolutionary War Patriot.* New York: Scholastic, Inc., 1998. A fictional diary of an orphan who works in a Boston tavern on the eve of the Revolution.

Forbes, Esther. *Johnny Tremain.* Boston: Houghton Mifflin, 1943. A novel set in Boston in 1773. A boy apprenticed to a silversmith becomes a messenger for a revolutionary group.

Fradin, Dennis Brindell. *Samuel Adams: The Father of American Independence.* New York: Clarion Books, 1998.

Gourley, Catherine. *Welcome to Felicity's World, 1774: Life in Colonial America.* Middleton, WI: Pleasant Company Publications, 1999.

North, Sterling. *George Washington, Frontier Colonel.* New York: Random House, 1957.

Olesky, Walter. *The Boston Tea Party.* New York: Franklin Watts, 1993.

Russell, Francis. *The French and Indian Wars.* New York: American Heritage Publishing Co., 1962.

Smith , Bradford. *Rogers' Rangers and the French and Indian War.* New York: Random House, 1956.

Smith, Carter, ed. *Daily Life: A Source Book on Colonial America.* Brookfield, CT: Millbrook Press, 1991.

Smith, Carter, ed. *The Revolutionary War: A Source Book on Colonial America.* Brookfield, CT: Millbrook Press, 1991.

Websites:

http://library.thinkquest.org/10966/
The Revolutionary War—A Journey Towards Freedom

ushistory.org/march/index.html
Virtual Marching Tour of the American Revolution

http://www.pbs.org/ktca/liberty/game/index.html
The Road to Revolution—A Revolutionary Game

http://www.pbs.org/ktca/liberty/chronicle/index.html
Chronicle of the Revolution
Read virtual newspapers of the Revolutionary era

http://www.vboston.com/VBoston/Content/FreedomTrail/Index.cfm
A virtual walking tour of Boston's Freedom Trail and its Revolutionary points of interest.

A Place to Visit:

Colonial Williamsburg, Williamsburg, Virginia. See how people lived in the Colonies before the Revolution.

About the Authors

James R. Arnold has written more than 20 books on military history topics and contributed to many others. Roberta Wiener has coauthored several books with Mr. Arnold and edited numerous educational books, including a children's encyclopedia. They live and farm in Virginia.

Set Index

Bold numbers refer to volumes; *italics* refer to illustrations

Acknowledgments

Architect of the Capitol: 42–43
Arizona Historical Society: 16–17,
Author's collection: 9, 38T
Eldridge S. Brooks, *The Century Book of the American Revolution*, 1897: 55
Anne S. K. Brown Military Collection, John Hay Library, Brown University, Providence, Rhode Island: 34–35, 36, 37, 61
Fishmongers' Company of London: 15 [*Custom House Quay* by Samuel Scott, 1757]
Library of Congress: Title page, 13T, 18, 19, 28, 34, 39T, 39B, 41, 42T, 46, 47T, 47B, 48, 49, 50, 52, 53T, 59, 62–63
Military Archive & Research Services, England: 30–31,
National Archives: 21, 22–23, 24, 25, 29T, 29B, 38B, 42B, 44–45, 51, 53B, 54T, 54B, 57, 60, 61T
National Guard Bureau: 32–33 [*Twenty Brave Men*, a National Guard Heritage painting by Jackson Walker]
National Park Service: Front cover, 40 [*The Boston Mob*, copyright Louis S. Glanzman]
State Historical Society of Wisconsin 26–27 [*Braddock's Defeat* by Edwin W. Deming, 1903]
U.S. Government Printing Office: 10–11, 12–13 by Don Trolani, 14, 58

Maps by Jerry Malone and Tim Kissel